Native American
Sports and Games

ROB STAEGER

Senior Consulting Editor Dr. Troy Johnson
Professor of History and American Indian Studies
California State University

MASON CREST PUBLISHERS • PHILADELPHIA

NATIVE AMERICAN LIFE

NATIVE AMERICAN LIFE

Native American
Sports and Games

ROB STAEGER

Senior Consulting Editor Dr. Troy Johnson
Professor of History and American Indian Studies
California State University

ACC-3096

MASON CREST PUBLISHERS • PHILADELPHIA

This book is dedicated to the athletes in my family—
my brothers, Ed, Tom, and Jim.

Mason Crest Publishers
370 Reed Road
Broomall, PA 19008
www.masoncrest.com

3 5 7 9 8 6 4 2

Library of Congress Cataloging-in-Publication Data

Staeger, Rob.
   Native American sports and games / Rob Staeger.
       p.   cm. — (Native American life)
Includes bibliographical references and index.
   ISBN: 1-59084-118-2
1. Indians—Sports—Juvenile literature.
2. Indians—Games—Juvenile literature. I. Title. II. Series.
E59.G3 S83 2003
                                                    2003266163

Frontispiece: Archery, an important skill for hunting and
warfare among Native Americans, was also a popular sport.

Table of Contents

Introduction

For hundreds of years the dominant image of the Native American has been that of a stoic warrior, often wearing a full-length eagle feather headdress, riding a horse in pursuit of the buffalo, or perhaps surrounding some unfortunate wagon train filled with innocent west-bound American settlers. Unfortunately there has been little written or made available to the general public to dispel this erroneous generalization. This misrepresentation has resulted in an image of native people that has been translated into books, movies, and television programs that have done little to look deeply into the native worldview, cosmology, and daily life. Not until the 1990 movie *Dances with Wolves* were native people portrayed as having a human persona. For the first time, native people could express humor, sorrow, love, hate, peace, and warfare. For the first time native people could express themselves in words other than "ugh" or "Yes, Kemo Sabe." This series has been written to provide a more accurate and encompassing journey into the world of the Native Americans.

When studying the native world of the Americas, it is extremely important to understand that there are few "universals" that apply across tribal boundaries. With over 500 nations and 300 language groups the worlds of the Native Americans were diverse. The traditions of one group may or may not have been shared by neighboring groups. Sports, games, dance, subsistence patterns, clothing, and religion differed—greatly in some instances. And although nearly all native groups observed festivals and ceremonies necessary to insure the renewal of their worlds, these too varied greatly.

Of equal importance to the breaking down of old myopic and stereotypic images is that the authors in this series credit Native

Americans with a sense of agency. Contrary to the views held by the Europeans who came to North and South America and established the United States, Canada, Mexico, and other nations, some Native American tribes had sophisticated political and governing structures— that of the member nations of the Iroquois League, for example. Europeans at first denied that native people had religions but rather "worshiped the devil," and demanded that Native Americans abandon their religions for the Christian worldview. The readers of this series will learn that native people had well-established religions, led by both men and women, long before the European invasion began in the 16th and 17th centuries.

Gender roles also come under scrutiny in this series. European settlers in the northeastern area of the present-day United States found it appalling that native women were "treated as drudges" and forced to do the men's work in the agricultural fields. They failed to understand, as the reader will see, that among this group the women owned the fields and scheduled the harvests. Europeans also failed to understand that Iroquois men were diplomats and controlled over one million square miles of fur-trapping area. While Iroquois men sat at the governing council, Iroquois clan matrons caucused with tribal members and told the men how to vote.

These are small examples of the material contained in this important series. The reader is encouraged to use the extended bibliographies provided with each book to expand his or her area of specific interest.

Dr. Troy Johnson
Professor of History and American Indian Studies
California State University

Native Americans played a variety of sports and games, as this illustration depicting a Florida tribe shows.

1 Native American Games

Two Penobscot Indian men gripped ropes, walking through the cold Maine countryside. The ropes were tied to a large log. They dragged the log through the snow behind them. Between their footprints, a wide path of flattened snow glistened in the sun. The men pulled the log down a steep hill and up and down a smaller one. They crossed a frozen lake, went a few yards farther, and stopped.

Back at the lodge, their sons were carving long branches. When the branches were smooth, they would be decorated to look like snakes. The snakes, thrown from the top of the hill, would slide down the track the men had just made. The air was crisp and cloudless. It was a good day to play snow snake.

Farther south, a Mandan warrior pulled back his bowstring. He pointed his arrow high into the air and let it fly. Like lightning, he grabbed another arrow and fired it. He followed that with another, and then another. His original arrow was still in the air when he fired a fifth and a sixth. He had just released his seventh arrow when his first arrow fell to the ground. He hoped seven would be enough to win the contest. Looking over at his competition, he wasn't sure.

On the other side of the continent, a Zuñi man batted a strange object into the air. It was a *shuttlecock*—a bundle of cornstalks with some feathers sticking out of it. Before it touched the ground, the man hit it into the air again. A friend watched him, counting the number of times he hit it. After he reached 83, the shuttlecock hit the ground. The second man picked it up and began bouncing it off his left hand. The first player started counting. There were two blankets on the ground nearby. The first man to reach 100 hits would win them both.

Far north of them, a group of Inuit men and women stood in a circle. They gripped a wide blanket made of stitched-together sealskin. They lowered it slightly, and a young girl climbed on and stepped into the center. On a count, the group shook the blanket, tossing the girl into the air. She did a flip and landed on her feet, laughing.

A Choctaw Indian in ballplayer's dress, painted in 1834.

Native Americans loved to play games. Men, women, and children all took part in them. Although boys and girls would often play together, it was rare for men and women to face each other in a game.

Games were played for many reasons. Some were played to cure disease. Others made the crops grow. Many games were played just for fun. Part of the fun was watching the sport and betting on the outcome.

The two competitors are neck
and neck in this illustration
depicting a Native American
canoe race.

The Native Americans played all sorts of games. They played ball games, such as *lacrosse*, and guessing games. They competed in *archery* and spear throwing. They loved to play dice games. Many sports passed from tribe to tribe. Some were popular throughout the country; others were unique to one place. Many of these games are similar to the games we play today.

Lacrosse, the sport for which the woodland
Indians of the Northeast were best known,
used a buckskin ball. Players' rackets were
made of bent saplings that had been netted
with leather thongs.

2 Games of the Northeast

The sport for which the woodland Indians are best known is lacrosse. This team game was popular throughout northeastern America. Lacrosse meant different things to the tribes that played it. To the Menomini in Wisconsin, it was a war game. They believed the legendary Thunderer god, Manidog, gave it to men. Playing it brought strength and skill in battle. In Ontario, the Huron believed the game helped heal the sick.

Legends said that a god, the Thunderer, invented lacrosse. Therefore, a man whose guardian spirit was the Thunderbird would call for a game. This man didn't play. He stayed on the sidelines as the game went on, praying and offering sacrifices. Before the game began, he would offer tobacco to the players. Then he chose the captains.

The captains picked their teams randomly. Every player had his own racket, which he decorated in his own way. Before the game, they would pile all their rackets together. One captain would be blindfolded. He would divide the rackets into two piles. These would be the two teams. The game was usually played with teams of five, but sometimes they swelled to as large as nine. Legends told of long-ago days when the game was played with nearly 100 people on each side.

Lacrosse rackets were made from **sapling** trees about four feet long.
The saplings were bent into oval loops at the ends. The loops were
then netted with leather thongs. The game was played on a field about
a quarter mile long. Two goalposts were set at each end. The object
was to get the ball between the posts. Each team had a goalie
protecting its goal. Some tribes, including the Ojibwa, used only one

Mandan archery contests, like the one shown here, often hinged not on accuracy but on distance or on how many arrows a participant could shoot in the air before the first one touched the ground.

Many tribes played variations of the game depicted in this painting. The object was to throw a spear or javelin through a rolling ring.

goalpost on each side. Players had to hit the goalpost with the ball or their racket. Players would move the ball up the field, passing it to each other. It was illegal to touch the ball with the hands—players could use only their rackets.

Lacrosse games were rough. It wasn't unusual for a player to break an arm or a leg, and bruises were expected. The games were played until a set number of goals was scored. It was usually five, but the game sponsor could change that when he began the game. Sometimes, a game would run all day. In many tribes, the sponsor gave a prize to each player who scored. The player would then give it to a woman on the sidelines. It was usually his aunt or another relative. After the game, they would give him a different prize.

Lacrosse originated as a religious ceremony, and it was often played as a contest between tribes. For many years, no one bet on lacrosse. As time passed, however, the game lost some of its religious significance and began to be played for fun. When this happened, people **wagered** on the winner. Some would even bet on each goal scored.

Only men played lacrosse. Women played a similar game called double ball. It was played with two **buckskin** balls joined by an eight-inch leather strap. Players could snag the double-ball strap with their sticks and pass it to their teammates. Team size and equipment varied. The sticks were usually curved and never had a pouch. The Potowatomi played with five to a side and one straight stick. Chippewa teams had more players. Each Chippewa player used two sticks, which were curved at the ends.

Double ball had a goalpost on each end of a 300-foot field, guarded by a goalie. The object of the game was to hit the post with the ball or a stick. As in lacrosse, gifts were awarded every time someone scored. The players would give their prizes to a man watching the game. He would repay them for the gifts later.

Men in the Northeast enjoyed many active games, such as

19

Lacrosse wasn't always played on a large field. In the winter, games were sometimes played on frozen lakes. The slippery ice made the game even rougher.

wrestling, foot racing, and bow shooting. One of their strangest games was the kick fight, played by the Menomini and Winnebago Indians. The game would start suddenly. Someone in a group would shout the game's name, *Ato'wi*, and the game would be on. Men would kick each other in the buttocks as hard as they could. When someone lost his temper or cried out in pain, he would drop out of the game. The winner was the man who could maintain his composure the longest.

A gentler game, though just as popular, was the **moccasin** game. Like a modern shell game, it was a guessing game that people gambled on. Someone would hide four stones in four different moccasins. One stone would be marked. The player would have to guess which moccasin the marked stone was in. While he guessed, onlookers sang a repetitive song.

This game varied among the tribes. In Kansas, the Potowatomi hid only one stone, rather than four. In some tribes, including the Chippewa, Winnebago, and Menomini, players used striking sticks to guess. The guesser would look at the moccasins carefully. When he thought he knew where the stone was, he would swat his choice with the stick.

Potowatomi men and women also gambled on dice games, but rarely together. A blanket would be spread out for throwing the dice. There were eight dice, carved from buffalo ribs. Six were circular disks with one colored side. Of the two remaining, one was shaped like a turtle, and another like a horse's head. Players would shake them in a basket and toss them onto the blanket. The roller would get points for how many dice came up the same color. Players used beans to keep score.

Some games spread across the country. Most Native Americans enjoyed games with hoops and poles. There were many different variations of the game, changing with the area. In New York, the Seneca called it the game of the **javelins**, or *ga-na-ga-o*. Two teams would line up, one on each side of a field. Each player had the same number of javelins. A six-inch hoop would be rolled in front of the first team's line. Players on the first team would try to throw their javelins through the hoop. The throwing team got to keep the javelins that made it through. Their opponents picked up the shots that missed.

Then, the hoop was rolled in front of the second team. They would all take a shot. Their misses would go to the first team. This would continue until one team had all the javelins.

21

Another throwing game was called snow snake. Many tribes played this game, although it was particularly popular among the Iroquois tribes. In the winter, men and boys would prepare ice ramps and tracks for playing the game. They would drag logs to make long channels in the snow. Some Iroquois tracks were a mile long.

Often, a crowd would gather around dice games. They would cheer, "Hub, hub, hub!" This noise is where we get the word *hubbub*, meaning a commotion.

A HISTORIC GAME

In 1763, a group of Ottawa Indians played lacrosse outside of Fort Michilmackinac in Michigan. The British soldiers inside the fort thought it was an innocent game. Then, someone knocked the ball near the gate of the fort. The players rushed to get it. Suddenly, the game changed. Instead of putting the ball in play, the players attacked the guards. They quickly overpowered them and swarmed inside. The entire fort was caught off guard. After the battle, the Ottawas took over the fort.

The Ottawa chief, Pontiac, had planned the clever sneak attack in advance. The fort's commanding officer had heard there would be a sneak attack. However, he ignored the report, thinking it was just a nervous rumor. That year, Pontiac took over nine English forts.

To play, players used hardwood sticks. The sticks, which could be anywhere from two to six feet long, were carved and decorated to look like a snake. Many would have a knob at one end, representing the head.

Players would balance the snake on one hand, steadying it with the other. They would run a few steps and flip the snake into the air. The snake would land and slide on the ice-covered track. The winner was the player whose snake slid the farthest. An experienced thrower could send his snake quite a long way! 𝕾

23

NATIVE AMERICAN LIFE

In the Southeast, lacrosse games often pitted
one village or tribe against another and
sometimes included hundreds of players. These
games could get quite rough.

3 Games of the Southeast

Few tribes played snow snake in the South. The climate was too warm for much snow. Many southeastern tribes, however, played lacrosse: Cherokee, Choctaw, Muskogee, and Seminole people all enjoyed the game. Like their northern neighbors, they took it quite seriously. The Cherokee considered games "the little brother of war." Nowhere was this attitude truer than in lacrosse.

Lacrosse was played from summer through the fall. Southeastern games involved even more ceremony than did those in the Northeast. Bands and villages would often challenge each other. Before their game, each competing village would hold a big dance ceremony. Men and women both danced, but they didn't touch. Instead, the players held their rackets. After the dance, players went to the river for a cleansing ritual. It was important to keep the exact part of the river they went to secret. Otherwise, the other team could put a curse on them by scattering their path with small pieces of rabbit.

Rabbits were considered *taboo* before a game, because they are easily frightened and confused. Players could not eat rabbit meat for at least a week, and sometimes a month, before a game. Several other things were also prohibited. Players couldn't eat frog, because frogs'

Two Native American ball teams gather around their goalposts while their women form lines for a ceremonial pregame dance.

bones are brittle. Babies are also fragile, so they had to be avoided, too. During that same time period, players could not touch a woman. This rule lasted for a week after the game as well. Needless to say, women were not allowed to touch the rackets.

The Natchez people in Louisiana played a game similar to modern horseshoes or lawn bowling. They called it the game of the pole. Two players would play. Each one carried a pole, about eight feet long. One would roll a ball onto the playing field. The ball was their target. Each player would throw his pole at the ball. Whoever got closest scored a point and rolled the ball for the next round.

Many other tribes of the Southeast played a similar game called chunkey. The best description of chunkey comes from the Mandan people of Missouri. Their games of chunkey were similar to the hoop and pole games of the North. In their case, they rolled a small stone ring, about three inches wide. The ring would still be moving when the players threw their poles. A perfect throw meant that the ring stopped around the tip of a pole.

A Cherokee man whose wife was pregnant was not allowed to play lacrosse. His strength was believed to be with his child.

They played on a smooth, clay court, so the pole would have a chance to slide. Still, this was an extremely difficult shot.

The artist George Catlin observed many games of Mandan chunkey. He wrote, "It is a game of great beauty, and fine bodily exercise, and these people have become excessively fascinated with it." This was true, to a horrible degree. Many chunkey players gambled themselves into poverty. Catlin reported that some players would "stake their liberty upon the issue of these games, offering themselves as slaves to their opponents in case they got beaten." Every so often, a player, devastated after a big loss, would even take his own life.

Another popular Mandan game was called the game of the arrow. This game also drew wagers, although not to the extremes of chunkey. Every player would put up a shield, a blanket, or some other valuable item as an entry fee. The winner would get everything at the end of the game. Unlike most archery competitions, accuracy was not important. In the game of the arrow, only speed counted. Archers would compete one at a time. The archer would fire an arrow into the air. Immediately, he would fire a second and a third. The object was to get the most

27

NATIVE AMERICAN LIFE

arrows into the air before the first one hit the ground. The fastest archers could get as many as eight arrows into the air at once.

Native Americans frequently gambled—on games of chance between two players or on the outcome of team competitions.

Not all of the games in the region were *strenuous* physical contests. Choctaw women played a lighthearted game that resembled jacks. The player would throw a ball into the air. She had to pick up a stick in time to catch the ball before it hit the ground. A player would continue until she had picked up all the playing sticks or missed catching the ball.

Choctaw men also enjoyed a dice game. Their dice were not like the ones made today. They used eight kernels of white corn as dice. One side of each kernel was charred black. This way, each die had two sides. The men would throw the dice and gain one point for each light side showing. All eight black sides up would count for eight points. The men bet on who would win the most points.

Another popular game was the ring and pin game. In a sense, it was a tiny, solitary game of chunkey. The equipment was a ring, or target, with a hole in it. Often, it was made from a bone, or several bones. It would be

A CHEROKEE LEGEND

Long ago, the four-legged animals challenged the birds to a lacrosse game. The animals had a good team. The fast deer, the strong bear, and the tough turtle were all ready to play. Some smaller animals also wanted to play, but the big ones wouldn't let them. So, two small mammals asked to play on the birds' team.

The birds would let them, but they needed to be able to fly. They made one of the animals a set of wings from drum leather. This is how the bat was born. Unfortunately, the birds didn't have enough leather for the other creature. Instead, they took his skin and stretched it out over his arms and legs. He became a flying squirrel.

Soon, the game began. The flying squirrel swooped down and grabbed the ball first. He scampered up a tree and gave the ball to the birds. The birds kept the ball in the air for a long while, but couldn't score. Eventually, one dropped the ball. The bat darted to the ground and caught the ball. He flew too fast for anyone, even the deer. He flew right to the goal and scored. Since then, bats and flying squirrels have been good luck for lacrosse players.

attached to a pin with a thin cord. Like chunkey, the object was to spear the ring with the pin. The player would throw the target into the air. As the target fell, he would try to catch it on the pin. Sometimes the target had several holes, each worth a different point value.

The Cheyenne called this a "love game." It was often used as a way of introducing young men and women. To strike up a conversation, single men would ask women if they would like to play. If a woman accepted, they could begin a courtship.

Ring and pin games were played across the continent, and the rules were similar. Most of the variation was due to the materials at hand or the number of holes in the target.

4 Games of the Northwest and Far North

When sports *migrate* from place to place, sometimes they have to be adapted to the environment. This was the case with lacrosse. The Inuit in Alaska played a variation of the game, with most of the same rules. However, wood was scarce. Instead of using netted wooden rackets, they played with netted baskets made from the sinew and bone of animals.

Several Inuit games depended on the materials they had on hand. One example is the blanket toss. This was a popular game, usually played at festivals. Seals or walrus hides would be stitched together to form the blanket. Only these materials had the strength needed for the game.

The blanket toss, a traditional game of the Inuit people, resembles gymnastics on a trampoline.

To play, a large group of people would grasp the blanket at all the edges, stretching it tight. Then, someone would climb onto the tight blanket. Once someone was in the center, the people at the edges would toss her into the air. The blanket behaved much like a modern trampoline. In some games, the object was to jump the highest. In others, people would do flips and somersaults before they landed. People took turns in the center while the others held the edges.

The Inuit people enjoyed several other jumping games. During seal hunts, seals would be tied together with an **avatuk**. This was a float made of sealskin, with rope on either end. It kept the dead seals from floating away. When the *avatuks* weren't in use, children used them to play *illupik,* a type of jump rope. Other games had players jumping as far as they could while holding their toes.

One game, called *aratsiaq,* combined jumping with aim. Players had to leap and kick a target hanging from a tree. Then they had to land on the foot that made the kick. After each player had a chance to kick it, the target would be raised. Players dropped out after they missed. In some games, players had to kick the target with both feet!

A game called spear the whale also involved a target hanging from a tree. In this case, the target was a diamond-shaped piece of bone with a circular hole in it. This was the "whale." It hung waist-high. Lines were drawn behind and in front of it, which the two players could not cross. The players stood on opposite sides of the "whale" and tried to spear the hole with 20-inch-long sticks. As they did this, they tried to prevent their opponent from doing the same. A block of wood usually dangled below the target, steadying it.

Another popular sport was wrestling. The Inuit had several versions. One type, called leg-twist wrestling, began with opponents lying on their sides facing each other. They would put their hands behind their knees and wrap their upper leg around their opponent's.

An Inuit from northern Canada competes in the "toe jump," which is like the broad jump except that the athlete must hold his toes when making his leap.

Then, using only their legs, they would try to flip each other over. In another wrestling game, the opponents stood with their feet flat on the ground. The object of this game was to lift the other person. Games of tug-of-war were also popular.

Another popular game in the Northwest was shuttlecock. The shuttlecock was a branch or piece of twig with feathers stuck into it. The game went by many names. The Kwakiutl people of British Columbia called it *quumla.*

Boys and girls both played *quumla,* although in the Skokomish tribe, girls tended to prefer it. Each player would have a wooden paddle, similar to a Ping-Pong paddle. The paddles were about a foot long and made out of thin boards. The children would stand in a circle. Using her paddle, the first player would bat the shuttlecock to her right. The next player had to hit it, keeping it moving around the circle. The object was to keep the shuttlecock in the air for the longest time.

When a player let the shuttlecock hit the ground, she dropped out of the circle. The game would continue in this

The object of this Inuit game, the "seal kick," is to touch the wooden seal with the feet. The competitor's legs are tied to his neck and the seal is raised after each round.

NATIVE AMERICAN LIFE

manner until another player let it drop. The circle would get smaller and smaller until there were just two players left. After that, the first one to miss ended the game.

Like the people of other regions, northern tribes played a version of the hoop and pole game. The Dakota people used a hoop a foot wide netted with leather thongs. The straps divided the hoop much like a modern dartboard. Players would get different amounts of points, depending on where their dart landed.

Children would form two teams. One team would roll the hoop, and the other would throw darts at it. When a player hit the heart, or center, of the hoop, he picked it up. Then, he would chase the other team. As they ran, he would swat them with the hoop. Players kept blankets nearby so they could wrap them over their backs and cushion the blows a little. After this, the next team threw the hoop, shouting "Ho! Here is a buffalo returning to you!"

The hand game was a popular game played by the Chinook and Clatsop tribes in Oregon. Almost every tribe played some form of this game. It's a simple game, so the fact that it traveled so far isn't too surprising. The game was a guessing game for two players. One would take a small stone and hide it in his hand. He would switch it from hand to hand, humming a simple tune. Then, the switching would end. The other player would bet that he knew which hand held the stone. Once the bet was made, he would guess. Games would go back and forth between hider and guesser.

Guessing games took other forms as well. People would put a variety of small wooden disks in two bags. Among the disks in one bag was a black disk; the other bag included a white disk. Players would choose black or white and then pick a bag. Also, sticks with unique designs would be placed in bundles of regular sticks. Players guessed which bundle held the right stick. These guessing games were usually played while singing a song of some sort. This helped to pass the time and increase the *suspense* while a player decided on his answer. ᔕ

37

NATIVE AMERICAN LIFE

Cat's cradle, still played today, was highly popular with the Hopi, Zuñi, and Navajo peoples of the American Southwest.

 **Games of the Southwest**

Although guessing games were popular in the North, generally only a few people played them at one time. In the Southwest, however, guessing games were a spectator sport. In New Mexico, the Zuñi games were so popular that people climbed onto rooftops to watch them. Different *clans* often challenged one another. Everyone came out to watch and cheer the players on. In one game, a stone ball would be hidden in one of four tubes. Players from opposite clans would have to guess which tube it was in. Correct guesses scored the clan points. This was a popular game for gamblers. Many valuable items—necklaces, *embroidery*, silver, and livestock—were won and lost on this game. Games usually lasted well into the night.

Another popular game is cat's cradle. This game is still played by children today. Players make patterns out of string wrapped around their fingers. This was popular throughout Native America, but particularly in the Southwest. The Navajo, Hopi, and Zuñi knew several patterns for the string. The Zuñi called the game *pishkappoa,* which means "netted shield." Legend says that the Zuñi creator, Spider Grandmother, taught the game to her twin sons, the war gods.

Spider Grandmother's web also figures in the Zuñi version of the hoop and pole game. The netted hoop represented the magical spider web woven by Spider Grandmother. It was played with corncob darts, but was otherwise much like the northern version.

The hoop and pole game isn't the only game that was popular on both sides of the Great Plains. Shinny was much like the Southeast's double ball. As with double ball, it was women who primarily played shinny, using curved sticks and buckskin balls. Some games were played for fun, but others were ceremonial. During a ceremonial game, the ball was sometimes filled with seeds. If it burst open during the game, the seeds would scatter around the field. This was a sign of a good harvest.

Another transplanted game was shuttlecock. The Zuñi called their game *po-ke-an,* and it was somewhat different from the northern variety. One of the differences was the shuttlecock itself. In the Southwest, it was made from corn husks and feathers, rather than wood. Also, no one used paddles in the Southwest. Instead, they hit the shuttlecock with their hands. Even the players were different. In the North, it was mostly a child's game. In the Southwest, grown men often played *po-ke-an.*

Po-ke-an also had different rules. A player would pick a number. He would bet that he could hit the shuttlecock that number of times without it touching the ground. He would bat the shuttlecock into

Native Americans, like highly
skilled riders everywhere, enjoyed
a good horse race.

This ceremonial race of the Mandan tribe involved circling around a barrel-like object, called the "big canoe," in the center of the village.

the air and use only one hand to keep it up. If he could hit the shuttlecock the right number of times, he would win the bet. If not, the other player would get a chance to match him. Whoever made it to the number first won the bet.

The shuttlecock game emphasized balance and control. The Hopi people played an archery game that stressed aim. The game played like a modern game of horseshoes. Before the game, players would build two slopes facing each other, about 200 feet apart. Each slope had a target for players to shoot at. The archer who came closest could take the first shot at the next target.

One Hopi arrow game didn't involve bows. Players would throw arrows to the ground instead. Each player would try to get the feathered back of his arrow, called the *fletching*, to lie across the other arrows. Whoever did could keep both arrows. This game was popular with Apache and Tewa children. Southwestern children also enjoyed playing with a wide variety of toys, including dolls, bean shooters, tops, hoops, darts, and small animals made from clay.

There was one type of game that was played all over the Southwest and nowhere else. This game was a ball race. It was a footrace, but with a twist. Teams of four or five players kicked objects from the starting point to the finish line. Often, the race would run through a set course, finally returning to the starting point. The course was sometimes 30 miles long.

Different tribes kicked different objects. The Pima and Tewa Indians used a stone ball. For the Opata, Mohave, and Yuma, the ball was made of wood. The Hopi used two cubes of hair stuck together. Some tribes used rings or wooden cylinders. The Bannock people even used an inflated cow bladder.

Whatever the object, it could not be touched by a racer's hands. Also, the race was run barefoot. If the ball was kicked into *briars* or sharp rocks, runners had to use their feet to get it back. It was obviously important to be careful. Any foot injuries would affect a player's running speed.

There were almost as many reasons to hold a ball race as there were objects to kick. The Zuñi ran the races after planting time. When the race was over, they would sacrifice the kicking sticks to their war god. The Keres people of New Mexico ran the race from March to May in order to bring rain. After some races, the objects would be buried to make the plants grow. Almost everywhere, people bet on the races. The bets could include money, bracelets, blankets, or livestock. Runners did not win prizes, but they would sometimes get a share of their friends' bets.

The most unusual game played in the Southwest was sometimes called the gallop race. It also had a more descriptive name: the chicken pull. At the start of some games, a rooster would be suspended from a pole. Another way to start was to bury the rooster in the ground so that only its head was showing.

BATTLE OF THE SEXES
One of the few contests in which men and women competed with each other was the rabbit hunt. Several southwestern tribes practiced this. A man and a woman would pair up and go hunting for rabbits together. If the woman shot the rabbit before the man did, they would switch clothes.

If this happened, the man had to shoot the next rabbit they saw. If the woman shot the next one instead, the man would have to bring her firewood.

At the beginning of the race, a player on horseback would grab the chicken, riding off with it. Other riders followed him. Everyone grabbed for the chicken. The game could get violent. Heedless of danger, players groped for the chicken while on horseback. Eventually, the chicken would be pulled apart. Players chased anyone who got a piece. They fought for the chicken as they all rode toward the finish line. The player who first reached the finish line with a piece of chicken won. Chicken pull was sometimes played on foot. This made it a bit safer, although the fights for chicken pieces were every bit as fierce.

45

NATIVE AMERICAN LIFE

This page from an Aztec codex, or manuscript book, depicts the dice game called **patolli**. The game was a favorite of serious gamblers: some even risked being sold into slavery if they lost!

# Games of Central and South America

The Indians of Central and South America lived differently from those to the north. Some groups became so powerful that they conquered other groups and built empires, with large cities. In such societies, different classes developed. The poor did much of the work to keep the empire going. The ruling classes, called the *elite*, had more time for games. Most of what we know of Aztec, Mayan, and Inca games comes from records of what the elite classes played. Commoners probably played similar games, but it is difficult to say for sure.

The Inca Empire flourished during the 12th through the 15th centuries in a large area in western South America that today includes much of Peru, Ecuador, and Chile. In Inca culture, games and ceremony were closely related. Upper-class maturity rites featured athletic contests. Footraces were run, and **mock** battles were staged. Team games tested boys' strength and endurance. Commoners were allowed to compete at some public celebrations. However, they didn't play the same games as the elite. Instead, they raced to see who could get the most manual labor done. People probably didn't look forward to this as much as a footrace or ball game.

When Chaco Indians played field hockey, they wore rows of sticks tied together with twine as shin guards.

Like tribes in North America, the Incas gambled on dice games. One popular game was called *ayllos.* It used ceramic and wood dice, marked with one to five points. Players would roll the dice, then move dried beans around a playing area. The dice throws determined the beans' movement.

Inca people gambled clothes and animals on *ayllos.* Tradition holds that the 10th Inca emperor bet considerably more. His son challenged him to a game, with a **province** as the prize. The emperor fell behind, and at the end of the game, he lost. The emperor agreed to let his son govern the province of Urcosuyo. From then on, the people of that region were called *Aylloscas,* in honor of the game.

The Mayan civilization flourished over a wide area in Central America—including territory that is today in southern Mexico, Belize, Guatemala, and Honduras—beginning about 400 B.C. The Mayans were still around when the Spanish arrived in the 16th century. As in the Inca Empire, common people in the Mayan world supported the upper classes, which included priests and the **nobility**. It is likely that, between feeding their families and growing food for the upper classes, Mayan farmers had relatively little time for recreation. Children also worked on the farms as soon as they were old enough. The Mayans did play some games, however. Many involved balls made from the gum of the rubber tree.

Mayans also used a rubber ball to play a game combining elements of basketball and soccer. This is probably the most famous Mayan game.

Participants in a traditional Mayan pole game get ready to perform. The four men, each with a long piece of rope attaching his ankle to the pole, will jump from the top and loop repeatedly around the pole.

A MAYA LEGEND

Long ago, there were two Mayan gods called the Hero Twins. They became famous ball players. One day, the god of death challenged them to play ball in the underworld of Xibalba. The Hero Twins agreed. They played many games against the death god, beating him every time.

The Hero Twins had only one problem. The death god would not let them leave. One day, one twin chopped off his brother's head. Then he picked up the head and put it back on his brother's neck. He lived! The death god was impressed. He asked the Hero Twins to try their trick on him. So they chopped off his head and left Xibalba. This is why a captive king on a losing ball team was decapitated.

The Hero Twins became the morning star and the sun. Every night, they return to Xibalba to play ball against the death god. When the sun and morning star rise, it is a sign they have escaped once again.

The Mayan ball game was played on a specially made court. Most cities had one. The court was shaped like a football field, although it was usually a bit smaller. It had two end zones and sloping stone walls on the two longer sides. A vertical ring was built into each wall.

The game was played with two teams. Each fought for control of a hard rubber ball a little bigger than a basketball. No one could touch the ball with his hands or feet. Players bounced the ball off of their hips, knees, chests, and heads. Points were scored if the opposing team touched the ball illegally, or if you could get the ball into the other team's end zone.

There was one other way to win the game. If the ball went through one of the vertical rings, the game ended at once. The

These are the ruins of an ancient handball court at Yagul, in Oxaca, Mexico. Spectators would sit on the sloped, stone-faced sides to watch the games.

team that made the shot would win, regardless of whether or not they were ahead at the time. The game could be won or lost in an instant. This was rare, but it did happen every so often. When it did, the winning team could chase the losers down and take their clothes and possessions.

The game changed as time went on. The sloping side walls moved to straight up-and-down. Also, the ball got smaller. Possibly, this was to make the ring shot easier and the games more unpredictable.

NATIVE AMERICAN LIFE

The Olmecs, an ancient people who created one of
the earliest civilizations in Mexico, carved these
enormous heads. Because of the headgear worn by
the sculpture, some archaeologists believe the statues
may have depicted ancient ball players.

One type of game was easy to predict. After a military victory, high-
ranking captives would be forced to play the game. They had no hope
of winning, as the game was fixed. After they lost, the captives were
sacrificed. If a king were among them, his head would be cut off. This

echoed the Hero Twins' decapitation of the death god in a Mayan legend.

Aztecs played a similar ball game called *tlachtli*. The court looked like a Mayan ball court, but with a line drawn down the middle. Like the Mayan game, players could not touch the ball with their hands or feet. Also, hits that did not go over the center line were fouls.

Aztecs also played a dice game called *patolli*. Some people became addicted to gambling on it. They carried the game mat and a bag of dice with them everywhere. Some **compulsive** gamblers even sold their children—and eventually themselves—into slavery.

Not every tribe in South America was part of an empire. Those that weren't had their own traditional games. Several different tribes lived in the Chaco plains in the center of South America. The natives of this area played some familiar games, such as snow snake, shuttlecock, and field hockey.

One of the Chaco Indians' favorite pastimes was boxing. Two lines of young men would enter the boxing area. A coach would lead each line. One boxer would break from his line and begin walking. Someone from the other line would step out to challenge him. They would circle each other. Then, with sudden fierceness, they would begin fighting. After a time, one of the coaches would stop the fight. Two other men would repeat the ritual, followed by two more. When every man had fought, the teams would march out in the same order in which they had entered.

Chaco children were trained to box at a young age. And men and women both boxed. Usually, men fought men and women fought women. However, one band of Chaco, the Payagua, allowed men and women to fight each other.

The Chaco also played a game that tested horsemanship and aim. Riders would gallop toward a ring hanging from a tree branch. They would have to put their sword through the ring to get a point.

Chaco children played a version of the ring and pin game. To play, they used 60 rings, connected by a string. They would throw the rings into the air and try to spear them with a stick. The player who caught the most rings on his stick won.

Another Chaco game was like a board game, using the ground as a board. Players would poke 21 holes into the ground in a semicircle pattern. The center hole was called the river. Each hole would have a small **counter** in it, representing a sheep. Each player would start with 10 sheep in his holes. Players would take turns rolling dice and moving a marker. This was usually an arrow stuck into the hole. They would cross the river to the other player's land. Players who landed on a sheep could steal it. The object was to steal all of the sheep.

The Caingang tribe of eastern Brazil enjoyed mock battles. A pile of clubs would be set up in an empty field. Two teams would gather on either side of the pile. They would then pick up clubs and throw them at each other. Women would run through the battle, defending themselves with thick bark shields. They would gather up the clubs and hand them to the men.

Sometimes, the clubs were replaced with torches. Needless to say, there were often injuries—and sometimes deaths—as a result of this game. However, everyone knew that it was a game, and no one tried to seek revenge for any accidents.

Native Americans have a long history of **sportsmanship**. There was rarely any cheating—especially in games in which it would be easy to cheat. Also, winning a contest was usually not regarded as a sign of superiority. An Odawa Indian named William Pelletier remembered the games of his childhood. He wrote, "If you beat someone by pulling a bow and arrow and shooting the arrow further, it only meant that you shot the arrow further at that moment. That's all it lasted. It didn't mean that you were better in any way whatsoever. It just meant that at that particular time the arrow went further; maybe it was just the way you let the bow go." In the end, playing the game was every bit as important as—and perhaps more important than—winning it. ◔

Chronology

400 B.C. Mayan culture of Central America begins.

A.D. 1300 Incas establish capital at Cuzco.

1325 Aztecs found their capital city, Tenochtitlán.

1492 Christopher Columbus sails to America in search of the Indies.

1521 The Spanish capture Tenochtitlán, conquering the Aztecs.

1524 The Spanish capture the Mayan city of Chichén Itzá.

1532 The Spanish conquer the Incas.

1620 Pilgrims settle at Plymouth, Massachusetts.

1626 The Dutch buy Manhattan Island from the Native Americans.

1763 Ottawa chief Pontiac attacks nine forts; this becomes known as Pontiac's Rebellion.

1766 A peace treaty ends Pontiac's rebellion.

1776 The United States of America wins its independence from England.

1804 The U.S. government enacts the Louisiana Territory Act, which tries to move southeastern Indians west of the Mississippi River.

1812 The War of 1812 begins; most Indians side with the British.

1813–14 The Creeks declare war on the United States; when the war ends the tribe loses 22 million acres of territory to the U.S. government.

1821 Sequoyah establishes the Cherokee alphabet.

1830 The U.S. government passes the Indian Removal Act; during the next eight year, Native Americans of the southeast are moved over the "Trail of Tears" to Oklahoma.

1867 The United States buys Alaska.

1876 On June 25, George A. Custer and his troops are killed by Sioux and Cheyene warriors at the Battle of the Little Bighorn.

1890 In December, the Seventh Cavalry kills 200 Sioux men, women, and children at Wounded Knee, South Dakota.

1907 Stewart Culin publishes a study of Native American games for the Smithsonian Institution.

2003 According to recent census estimates, there are more than 3 million Native Americans living in the United States and Canada.

NATIVE AMERICAN LIFE

Glossary

archery the practice of shooting with a bow and arrows.

avatuk a float made of sealskin, with rope on either end, used during seal hunts.

briar a thorny wild plant.

buckskin the skin of a male deer, usually made into a soft, pliable leather.

clan a group of people tracing descent from a common ancestor.

compulsive caused by a psychological obsession.

counter a small object used in games to mark a player's position or to keep score.

elite a small group of people within a larger group who have more power, social standing, wealth, or talent than the rest of the group.

embroidery something ornamented with decorated needlework.

fletching the feathered back of an arrow.

javelin a light spear thrown as a weapon of war or in hunting.

lacrosse a team sport played with a ball and rackets with netted pouches.

migrate to move from one country or locality to another.

moccasin a soft, leather shoe that has no heel.

mock having the character of an imitation.

nobility people who belong to an aristocratic social or political class.

province an administrative district or division of a country.

sapling a young tree.

shuttlecock a small rounded object, often including feathers, used in Native American games; a similar item is used in the modern game badminton.

sportsmanship good conduct by a participant in a sport or game, including observance of the rules or fair play, respect for others, and graciousness in losing.

strenuous requiring great energy, strength, stamina, or effort.

suspense a feeling of tense excitement about how something will end.

taboo forbidden.

wager to bet or gamble.

Further Reading

Culin, Stewart. *Games of the North American Indians, Volume 1: Games of Chance.* Lincoln: University of Nebraska Press, 1992.

——. *Games of the North American Indians, Volume 2: Games of Skill.* Lincoln: University of Nebraska Press, 1992.

Fagan, Brian M. *The Aztecs.* New York: W. H. Freeman and Co., 1984.

Glatzer, Jenna. *Native American Festivals and Ceremonies.* Philadelphia: Mason Crest, 2003.

Moulton, Candy. *Everyday Life Among the American Indians.* Cincinnati, Ohio: Writer's Digest Books, 2001.

Sharer, Robert J. *Daily Life in Maya Civilization.* Westport, Conn.: Greenwood Press, 1996.

White, John Manchip. *Everyday Life of the North American Indians.* New York: Dorset Press, 1988.

Internet Resources

http://www.ahs.uwaterloo.ca/~museum/
The Elliott Avedon Museum and Archive of Games contains information on several games played by the Native Americans.

http://www.nativetech.org/games/
This site contains information on Native American technology and art.

http://www.hickoksports.com/history.shtml
A history of sports, including several played by Native Americans.

http://oneida-nation.net/lacrosse.html
This site describes the game of lacrosse as it was played by the Oneida.

Index

Picture Credits

Contributors

Dr. Troy Johnson is a Professor of American Indian Studies and History at California State University, Long Beach, California. He is an internationally published author and is the author, co-author, or editor of fifteen books, including *Contemporary Political Issues of the American Indian* (1999), *Red Power: The American Indians' Fight for Freedom* (1999), *American Indian Activism: Alcatraz to the Longest Walk* (1997), and *The Occupation of Alcatraz Island: Indian Self-Determination and the Rise of Indian Activism* (1996). He has published numerous scholarly articles, has spoken at conferences across the United States, and is a member of the editorial board of the journals *American Indian Culture and Research* and *The History Teacher.* Dr. Johnson has served as president of the Society of History Education since 2001. He has been profiled in *Reference Encyclopedia of the American Indian* (2000) and *Directory of American Scholars* (2000). He has won awards for his permanent exhibit at Alcatraz Island; he also was named Most Valuable Professor of the Year by California State University, Long Beach, in 1997. He served as associate director and historical consultant on the PBS documentary film *Alcatraz Is Not an Island* (1999), which won first prize at the 26th annual American Indian Film Festival and was screened at the Sundance Film Festival in 2001. Dr. Johnson lives in Long Beach, California.

Rob Staeger lives and writes near Philadelphia. A former newspaper editor, he has written many short stories for young people and several plays for older ones. He has written several nonfiction books, including *Wyatt Earp*, *Boom Towns*, and *Native American Hunting.*